TABLE OF CONTENTS

OUR WORLD IN PICTURES

THE EARTH

AN INTRODUCTION FOR CHILDREN FROM 6 TO 10

Conception
Émilie BEAUMONT

Text
Agnès VANDEWIELE

Images
Vincent JAGERSCHMIDT
François RUYER

Translation
Lara M. ANDAHAZY

FLEURUS

OUR PLACE IN THE UNIVERSE

Scientists now think that the universe was formed about 15 billion years ago. It started with the Big Bang when a small but very dense mass of matter exploded. The gas and particles projected in every direction formed countless groups of stars, the galaxies. Then, about 5 billion years ago, one of these spinning clouds of gas and dust contracted and produced our solar system. First it formed a disk then a ball which became our Sun. Other parts of the cloud formed the planets and their satellites such as Earth and the Moon about 4.5 billion years ago.

HOW THE EARTH WAS FORMED

A huge cloud of gas (A) produced bits of matter as it contracted. These bits came together and formed the Sun, Earth and the other planets (B). It took Earth 4100 million years to become a ball of rock (C). In the beginning, Earth was very hot. It cooled down very slowly. (D). Other bits of matter came together to make the Moon (E). It is Earth's satellite.

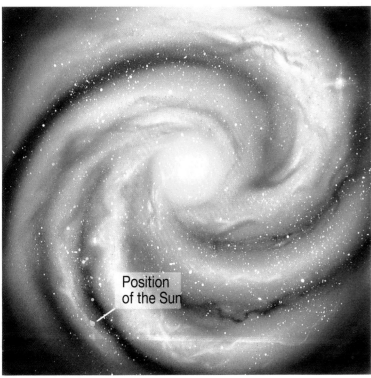

THE MILKY WAY

The universe contains billions of galaxies. Earth and our solar system are part of one called the Milky Way. This galaxy contains billions of stars and is shaped rather like a giant spinning plate. It takes 250 million years for it to spin around once. Our solar system is on the edge of the disk and turns with it.

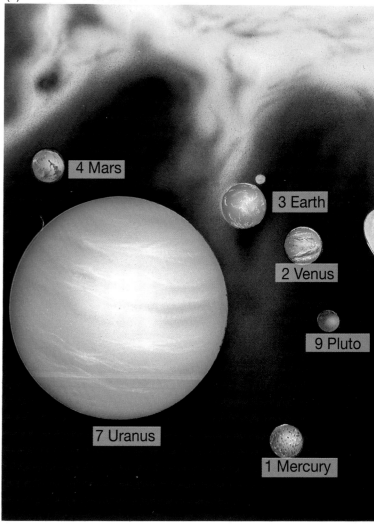

THE PLANETS

The nine different planets in our solar system are, starting closest to the Sun, Mercury, Venus (closest to Earth), Earth, and then Mars (with its red soil). Further out are bigger planets that have rings and satellites. They are Jupiter (the biggest of all), Saturn, Uranus and Neptune. The planet furthest from the Sun is tiny Pluto covered with frozen gas. Earth is the only planet with life on it.

Sun

1

2

3

4

5

6

7

8

9

ORBITING PLANETS

These nine planets orbit around the Sun on oval-shaped paths. The further away they are, the longer it takes them to go around the Sun. It takes Mercury (the closest to the Sun) 88 days. It takes Pluto (the furthest from the Sun) 247.7 years.
1 Mercury - 2 Venus - 3 Earth - 4 Mars - 5 Jupiter - 6 Saturn - 7 Uranus - 8 Neptune - 9 Pluto

Sun

5 Jupiter

6 Saturn

8 Neptune

IMAGES OF EARTH

Centuries ago, we thought that Earth was flat like a plate and situated in the center of the universe. Pythagoras (in the sixth century B.C.) and then Ptolemy discovered that Earth is round. But it took the navigator Magellan to prove it by sailing all the way around the world (in 1519-1522). A short time later, Copernicus and Galileo proved that Earth was not the center of the universe but that it and the other planets move around the Sun. Little by little astronomers and scientists got a clearer image of the shape of Earth and its movement around the Sun. Telescopes, radars, photos and satellites let us draw very accurate maps, even of places we can not go.

Copernicus

Galileo

COPERNICUS AND GALILEO

In 1506, Copernicus, a Polish astronomer, thought that the Sun stayed in place and Earth moved around it. Galileo, an Italian, built astronomical telescopes to let us see things far away. With them he proved that Earth really does move around the Sun.

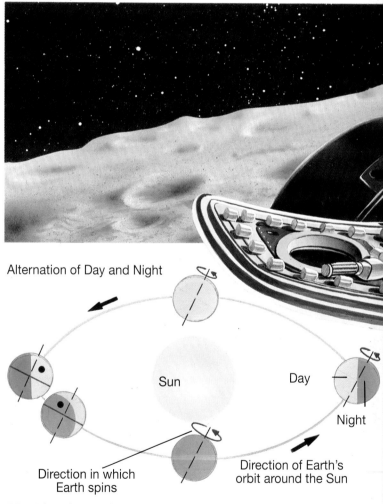

Alternation of Day and Night

Sun

Day

Night

Direction in which Earth spins

Direction of Earth's orbit around the Sun

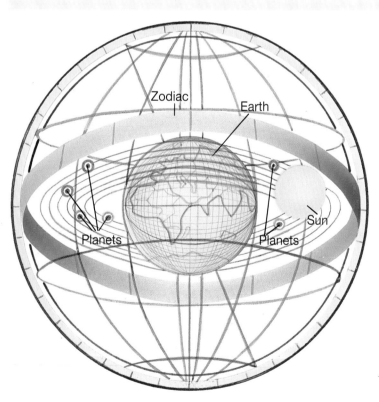

PTOLEMY'S SYSTEM

Ptolemy (a great Greek astronomer who lived in the second century A.D.) thought that Earth was the center of the universe and surrounded by air and fire. Each of the 6 known planets and the Sun moved around Earth, each in a separate sphere. His theory was called into question much later by Copernicus.

EARTH'S ROTATION AROUND THE SUN

It takes Earth one day and night, exactly 23 hours, 56 minutes and 4 seconds, to spin around once. Each day, any one place on the earth moves from where it gets light from the Sun to being in the shade (night). It takes Earth one year, exactly 365 days and 6 hours, to go around the Sun once. It covers more than 580 million miles at a speed of more than 18 miles per second!

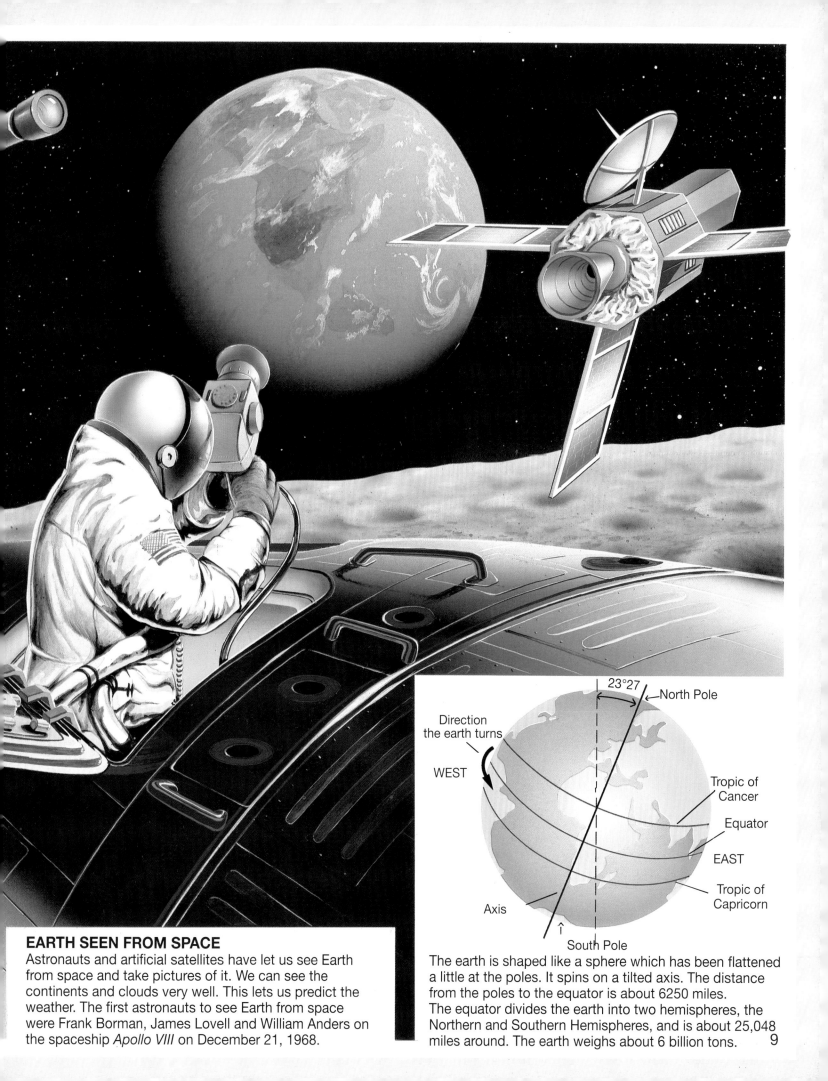

23°27′ North Pole

Direction
the earth turns

WEST

Tropic of
Cancer

Equator

EAST

Tropic of
Capricorn

Axis

South Pole

EARTH SEEN FROM SPACE

Astronauts and artificial satellites have let us see Earth
from space and take pictures of it. We can see the
continents and clouds very well. This lets us predict the
weather. The first astronauts to see Earth from space
were Frank Borman, James Lovell and William Anders on
the spaceship *Apollo VIII* on December 21, 1968.

The earth is shaped like a sphere which has been flattened
a little at the poles. It spins on a tilted axis. The distance
from the poles to the equator is about 6250 miles.
The equator divides the earth into two hemispheres, the
Northern and Southern Hemispheres, and is about 25,048
miles around. The earth weighs about 6 billion tons.

THE EARTH'S WEALTH

Our planet seems very big to us but it is only a little more than 3,900 miles from the surface to the center of the earth. The ground under our feet is made up of different rocks like limestone and granite. The earth and its oceans are full of wealth: all the metals (iron, nickel, copper, aluminum, gold, etc.) used by industry, as well as many carbon, oil and natural gas deposits. Oil was first formed in the sea. Tiny algae and animals fermented for millions of years to make it. Like natural gas, oil is found in underground pockets or under the oceans.

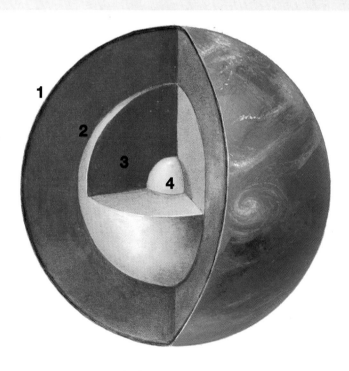

WHAT IS THE EARTH MADE OF?

The earth is made up of different layers like a big onion. First there is the crust (1) which is about 6 to 25 miles thick. It floats on a thick fluid layer called the mantle (2) made up of iron and magnesium. The mantle is about 1,800 miles thick. Next comes the external core (3). It is liquid and goes down to about 3,125 miles deep. In the very center is the internal core (4) made up of iron and nickel. We think it is solid despite its very hot temperature—more than 6,500°F!

An Opencast Mine

In this Australian iron mine, the veins of iron are on the surface of the earth. The ore is ground up and then taken to steelworks. In the steelworks the iron is extracted and transformed into cast iron and steel. We use these metals to make buildings, ships, cars and machines.

There are about 30,000 oil fields being used in the world. But 80% of the world's oil comes from only 200 of them. The biggest oil fields are in Saudi Arabia, Kuwait, and Venezuela.

The crude oil that comes out of the earth can not be used as it is. It has to be refined in order to become gasoline, heating oil, diesel oil and other petroleum products that are used to make lots of things like plastic.

Close to 20% of the energy used in Europe comes from the gas deposits and oil fields in the North Sea. Each oil field is drilled from an oil platform.

PRECIOUS ROCKS AND GEMS

Ruby   **Sapphire**   **Diamond**

Precious gems are natural minerals found in rocks.
We cut them to make jewelry.

Basalt   **Granite**   **Slate**

Basalt and granite come from molten rock in the depths of the earth that gets thrown to the surface and cools.
Slate is a sedimentary rock that was under lots of pressure for centuries. Slate is cut up in sheets to cover roofs.

Oolitic and Organic Limestone

They are sedimentary rocks created by the accumulation of sediment: sand (oolitic limestone) or living organisms (organic limestone).

11

THE BEGINNINGS OF LIFE

When the earth was formed 4.5 billion years ago, there was no sign of life yet. Life began in the warm seas 3.8 billion years ago. The first living organisms were made up of a few cells like algae. Invertebrates appeared next followed by fish. Some of them left the water and became amphibians living both in and out of the water. Then reptiles colonized the land and skies. Some were the ancestors of the dinosaurs who ruled the earth for more than 140 million years. When the dinosaurs died out, birds and mammals took over the earth.

6 - The first dinosaurs appeared about this time (230 million years ago). They were to become the masters of the earth. Some were carnivores and others were herbivores. The Tyrannosaurus (2) was a carnivorous monster 36 feet long and more than 18 feet tall! Dinosaurs disappeared 65 million years ago.

MAMMOTHS

Mammoths lived during the Great Ice Age 2 million years ago. Their thick fur protected them from the cold. They disappeared only 10,000 years ago. Prehistoric man hunted them.

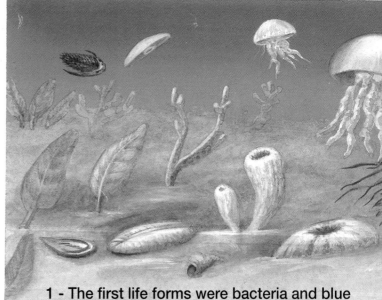

1 - The first life forms were bacteria and blue algae. Then, 600 million years ago, the first invertebrates appeared: worms, coral, sponges, mollusks, jelly fish and sea feathers.

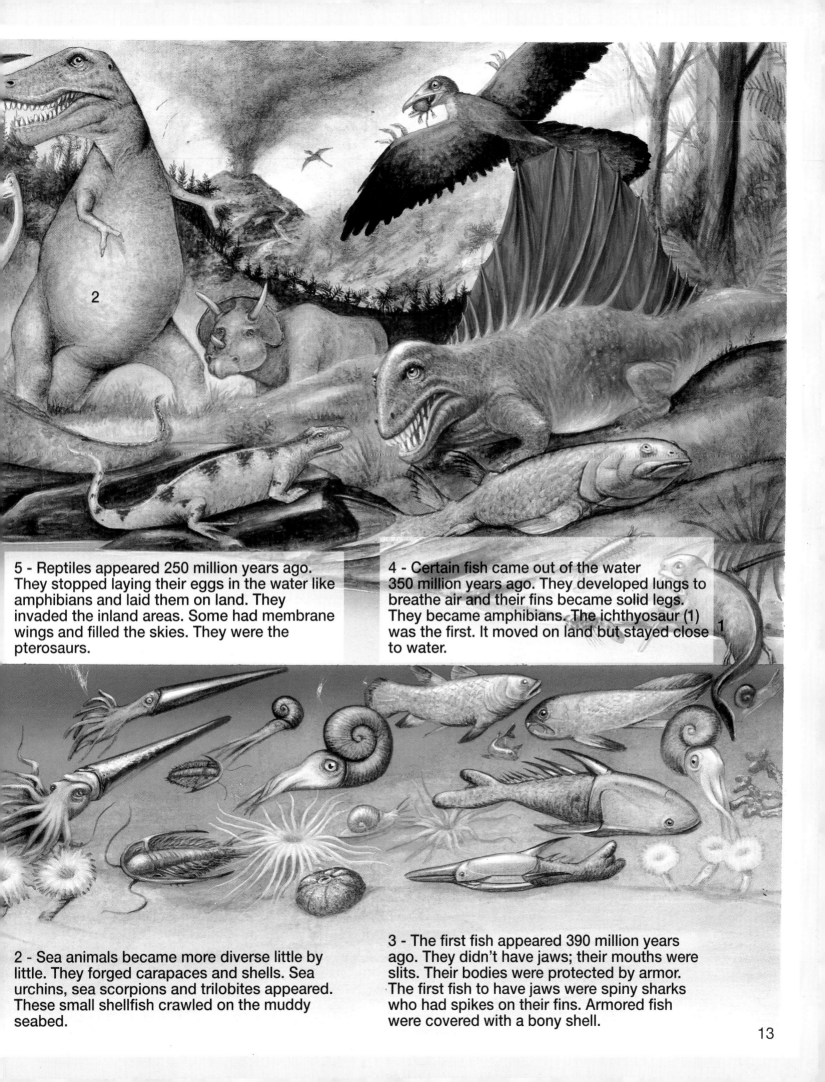

5 - Reptiles appeared 250 million years ago. They stopped laying their eggs in the water like amphibians and laid them on land. They invaded the inland areas. Some had membrane wings and filled the skies. They were the pterosaurs.

4 - Certain fish came out of the water 350 million years ago. They developed lungs to breathe air and their fins became solid legs. They became amphibians. The ichthyosaur (1) was the first. It moved on land but stayed close to water.

2 - Sea animals became more diverse little by little. They forged carapaces and shells. Sea urchins, sea scorpions and trilobites appeared. These small shellfish crawled on the muddy seabed.

3 - The first fish appeared 390 million years ago. They didn't have jaws; their mouths were slits. Their bodies were protected by armor. The first fish to have jaws were spiny sharks who had spikes on their fins. Armored fish were covered with a bony shell.

THE FIRST MEN

The skeleton of Lucy, the first humanoid to walk upright, was discovered in Ethiopia in 1974. This young Australopithecus is thought to have lived 3 million years ago. Homo habilis, the first real human, appeared 2.5 million years ago. His brain was bigger and he was more skilful and more intelligent. Homo erectus, who discovered fire, left Africa and adapted to new climates. They traveled to the Near East, China and Europe. Next came Neanderthal man. They lived in well organized societies and buried their dead. Finally, Cro-Magnon man perfected language. We descend from these early humans.

AUSTRALOPITHECUS

These humanoids lived in East and Southern Africa. They spent part of their time on the ground and part of their time in trees. They ate fruit, roots and leaves. They made the first tools, stones with sharp edges.

NEANDERTHAL MAN

They built huts to protect themselves from the cold during the Ice Age in Eastern Europe. Their huts were made of skins stretched across mammoth bones or tusks. They hunted cave bears, mammoths and reindeer.

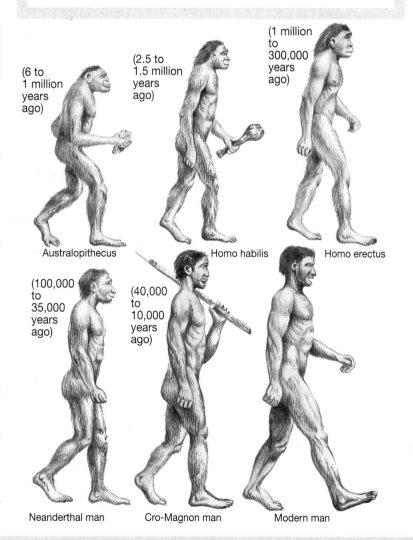

(6 to 1 million years ago)

(2.5 to 1.5 million years ago)

(1 million to 300,000 years ago)

Australopithecus

Homo habilis

Homo erectus

(100,000 to 35,000 years ago)

(40,000 to 10,000 years ago)

Neanderthal man

Cro-Magnon man

Modern man

HOMO HABILIS

These men lived in savannas and hunted all sorts of small animals (frogs and chameleons) as well as gazelle. They were clever and made better tools to cut meat and scrape the skins of the animals they killed. They built the first huts.

HOMO ERECTUS

500,000 years ago these men managed to master fire. Fire let them cook their food, stay warm and harden the points of their weapons and tools. It also helped keep wild animals away. They invented a new tool, the ax. It was a very sharp piece of flint hewn on both sides.

CRO-MAGNON MAN

They lived in caves and painted pictures of animals on the cave walls. They used animal hair brushes and brown and yellow ocher earth to paint. They also carved small statues out of bones and clay and made jewelry. They sewed clothes out of animal skins and fur using bone needles.

SEAS AND OCEANS

Earth is called "the blue planet" because two thirds of its surface is covered with water. It has hundreds of seas and five oceans. The largest is the Pacific Ocean; it covers 70 million square miles. Most sea water is salty. The largest amount of fresh water is in the Antarctic in the form of huge blocks of ice or icebergs that are moving towards the ocean.

The ocean bed is covered with plains, mountains and deep canyons like the land. The deepest is the Marianne Abyss in the Pacific Ocean. It is more than 33,000 feet deep.

Storms

When a mass of air in one area is under high pressure it rushes into areas where the air is under less pressure. The wind created by this movement causes storms. A force 12 wind (more than 80 miles per hour) can raise 45-feet-high waves. Squalls and waves toss ships around and put them in danger.

When the earth was first formed it didn't have seas or oceans. It was a ball of fire. When it cooled down the large clouds surrounding it shed their water and filled the low areas to form the first seas.

The Difference Between Seas and Oceans

Oceans are huge and seas are smaller and often surrounded by land. There are five oceans. The Indian Ocean is between Africa and the South Sea Islands (Oceania). It stretches to the shores of India. The Atlantic Ocean is between America and Europe and Africa. The Pacific covers a third of the globe between Asia and Oceania and America. It is the deepest ocean. The Arctic and Antarctic Oceans surround the North and South Poles. The largest seas are the Mediterranean Sea, the North Sea, the Red Sea and the Caspian Sea. The smallest are the Dead Sea (between Israel and Jordan) and the Aral Sea north of Turkestan.

Very violent storms are called cyclones in the Indian Ocean, hurricanes in the West Indies and typhoons in South East Asia.

Fishing

The seas and oceans are filled with fish. There are more than 25,000 different species of fish living in cold and warm waters. Many populations eat mostly fish.

Tides

You can see the ocean rise and fall on the coasts. These are tides caused by the pull of the Sun and especially the Moon on the water. The Moon pulls twice as hard as the Sun. But the height of the tides also depends on the coastline and the depth of the sea bottom. In Mont-Saint-Michel in France high tide reaches 36 feet. Tides vary a lot from one area to another. On the European coast high tide comes 6 hours after low tide; there are two high and two low tides per day. Vietnam has only one high tide per day.

OUR CHANGING EARTH

The earth's surface is made up of moving plates. These mobile plates slide on the thick mantel layer and cause continental drift.
Earthquakes occur when these plates get closer together or further apart. There is an earthquake somewhere on the planet every 30 seconds. Many of these earthquakes happen at the bottom of the oceans or in deserts. Volcanoes are formed when magma makes its way to the surface and spits out through a crack in the crust. There are about 10,000 volcanoes on Earth. The tallest are in Hawaii and are up to 12,000 feet high.

An Underwater Volcano

Many volcanoes are formed under water. We don't usually see them but sometimes they gush out of the water. This makes a spectacular sight and forms a new island. For example, on November 14, 1963, a volcano erupted off the coast of Iceland. Gigantic amounts of water, dust and burning gas gushed out of the ocean for more than a week. Then, a crater formed and a new volcanic island was born. It was named Surtsey. It grew to over one square mile in three years.

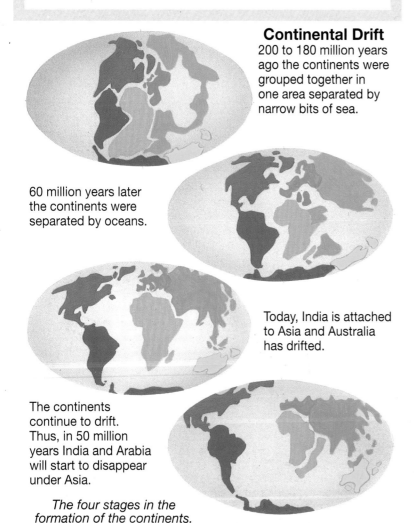

Continental Drift

200 to 180 million years ago the continents were grouped together in one area separated by narrow bits of sea.

60 million years later the continents were separated by oceans.

Today, India is attached to Asia and Australia has drifted.

The continents continue to drift. Thus, in 50 million years India and Arabia will start to disappear under Asia.

The four stages in the formation of the continents.

A Volcanic Eruption

Volcanoes are made up of layers of hardened lava and ash. When volcanoes erupt burning gas pushes magma up from the depths of the earth through the chimney to the surface. The magma that comes out of the crater is called lava. Lava is thrown into the air surrounded by a cloud of ash and gas. It also flows down the sides of the volcano.

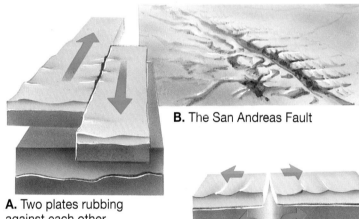

Firemen after an earthquake

Earthquakes

The biggest earthquakes happen where plates meet. The cracks that open up in the ground swallow up cars, destroy buildings and injure many people. Firemen and rescue teams help survivors trapped under the ruins.

B. The San Andreas Fault

A. Two plates rubbing against each other

C. Two plates moving apart

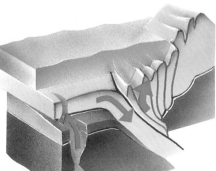

D. One plate sliding under another

Moving Plates

When two plates rub against each other (A) they create faults like the 600 mile long San Andreas fault in California (B). When two plates move apart (C) they cause a crack. Rocks coming up out of such a crack formed an underwater mountain range in the middle of the Atlantic Ocean called the Mid-Atlantic Ridge. Plates can also move under neighboring plates and lift up and tear them (D). Mountains and volcanoes grow up through the cracks. Two examples are the Andes and the Himalayas.

19

LANDFORMS

There are a lot of different landscapes on Earth: mountains, plains, valleys, rocky coastlines, etc. These different landforms are caused by the movement of the earth's crust and erosion.

When the plates that make up the earth's crust run into each other the edges raise up and form mountains. Then, wind, rain and snow slowly wear down the summit and streams dig valleys. These changes are very slow and can't be seen with the naked eye.

The Himalayas and the Alps are fairly new mountains and are still growing (less than an eight of an inch per year).

THE GRAND CANYON IN ARIZONA
The Colorado River dug deeply into the rock in Arizona to make its bed. The Grand Canyon is 277 miles long, varying between 5 and 15 miles wide and 6000 feet deep in some parts. The river flows below sea level in some places.

GLACIERS
Snow clumps together and turns into ice at high altitudes. This creates glaciers that move very slowly down the mountains. They tear chunks of rock off the mountainsides. Over centuries, some of these fragments polish the glacier bed and dig valleys.

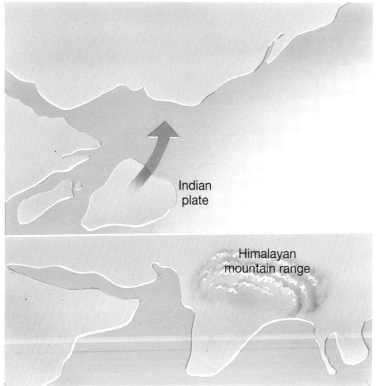

Indian plate

Himalayan mountain range

THE FORMATION OF THE HIMALAYAS
India used to be separate from Asia but 45 million years ago it moved closer. The Indian plate and the Asian plate crashed into each other and created a huge mountain chain, the Himalayas. The tallest mountain in the world is Mount Everest (29,028 feet) in the Himalayas.

chasms

stalactites

galleries

stalagmites

limestone pillars

underground water

water resurfaces

CAVES

Caves and underground rivers are caused by rainwater seeping into limestone. It takes many thousand years for a cave to be formed. In the beginning water seeps in through small cracks that get wider little by little and digs deep holes.

THE BIRTH OF MOUNTAINS

Powerful currents of molten matter under the earth's crust push up the mantel. The pressure forces the rocks on the surface to fold and lift up. This forms mountains. This is how the Himalayas and Alps grew at a rate of 8 inches to 3 feet every thousand years.

CLIFFS

The oceans and seas change the coastline. Waves wear away the base of chalk cliffs and rip off pieces of rock. The rocks are worn down by the movement of the waves and become pebbles.

COUNTRIES AND THEIR PEOPLE

Mankind lives everywhere life is possible on Earth. There are lots of very different peoples and countries. Each has its own language (more than 300 different languages are spoken around the world!), customs, religion, way of life, type of food and fashion. There is a huge difference between the lives of an American business man and a Chinese farmer! Some countries like China and India are overpopulated. Other areas like the Antarctic are almost empty. The population of the earth is constantly growing. 2,000 years ago there were 250 million people, in our day there are 5.5 billion and there will be 7 billion in the year 2010!

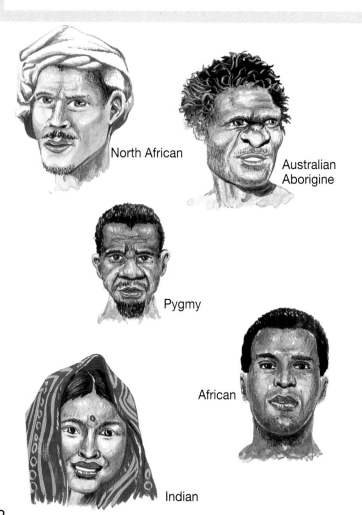

North African

Australian Aborigine

Pygmy

African

Indian

NEW YORK, THE MELTING POT

Immigrants from the four corners of the world live in New York. They come from more than 164 different countries and speak all kinds of languages. The largest immigrant groups include people from Italy, China, Poland, Russia and Puerto Rico. This makes New York an exciting place.

MEXICO CITY

This gigantic city contains more than 20 million people. It is easily the largest city in the world and is constantly growing. There is so much traffic that the air is very polluted. The suburbs surrounding the city are very poor.

POLYNESIA

Traditionally, Polynesians lived mostly from fishing and built canoes out of tree trunks and roofed their huts with coconut palms. Some still do. They eat mostly fish and fruits and vegetables.

ESKIMOS

Eskimos live near the North Pole in small wooden houses. When they go hunting or fishing they sometimes sleep in igloos. They wear seal skin and caribou fur coats to protect themselves from the cold.

EUROPE

Northern Europeans tend to be blond and light skinned. In Southern Europe people tend to have dark hair and skin. Over the centuries European peoples mixed together and today Europeans are very diverse people.

CHINA, OVERPOPULATED

One person out of four on Earth is Chinese. 1.2 billion people live in China. There are too many people so now each family in China can have only one child. The streets are very crowded and most people ride bicycles.

AN AFRICAN MARKETPLACE

African marketplaces are lively. You can find sweet potatoes, cassava roots, papayas, mangoes, coconuts and antelope meat. African women often wear colorful dresses called bubus and carry their babies on their backs.

THE GANGES, A SACRED RIVER

In the city of Varanasi in India, Hindus bathe in the Ganges river to purify themselves. They venerate this sacred river. India has the most religious celebrations in the world for thousands of gods. Some last several days.

FLORA AND FAUNA

Millions of different animals and plants evolved and multiplied across the earth according to the landscape and climate. The amount of water and the temperature are the main factors in their distribution. In the Amazon forest it is hot and humid all year long and the biggest variety of flora and fauna is found there. Animals adapt to the climate and vegetation available for them to eat. In deserts it is often more than 120°F and many animals like the scorpion spend the day in a hole and come out at night. In the savannas elephants and giraffes follow the rain which brings the plants they eat.

Mountains

The flora at high altitudes is mostly evergreen trees and plants that can stand cold temperatures. Marmots (1) fight the cold by hibernating in dens. Mountain goats (2) and ibex (3) have hooves that are adapted to climbing.

Temperate Regions

Insects are plentiful in prairies dotted with flowers. Birds make nests in trees and hedges. Some birds migrate south for the winter where it is warmer. Stags graze on prairie grasses; wild boars eat roots and mushrooms.

Deserts

Desert plants and animals are adapted to hot weather. Dromedaries and camels can go a few weeks without drinking thanks to their humps of fat that store energy when food and water are scarce. Plants have very deep roots or, like cactuses in American deserts, store water in their leaves.

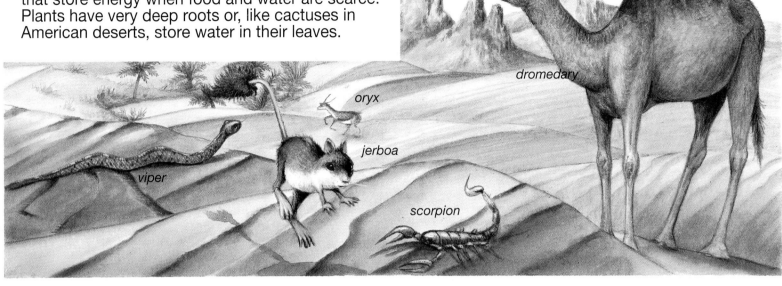

oryx

jerboa

viper

scorpion

dromedary

Tropical Forests

All sorts of wild animals live among the giant trees and tangled vines: gorillas, snakes, parakeets, etc. Many of them eat the leaves, fruits and flowers that grow in plenty on the trees.

The Antarctic

Colonies of penguins (1) live on the ice floes; seals (2), sea elephants (3) and finbacks (4) live in Antarctic waters. In summertime, penguins fill up on fish, shrimp and squid. They fatten up to survive the glacial winters.

CLIMATES

The climate of a region comes from its temperature (how much sun it gets), its humidity, the water cycle and the wind. There are all kinds of climates between the North Pole (where the winters are long and cold) and the equator (where it is hot and damp). The climate of any one area does not only come from its place on the globe. Altitude plays a role too. High mountain tops are covered in snow all year long even in temperate regions. The oceans also affect areas close to them. Ocean currents warm the coasts. Far from oceans in the center of continents the climate is more severe like in Siberia or the Saharan Desert.

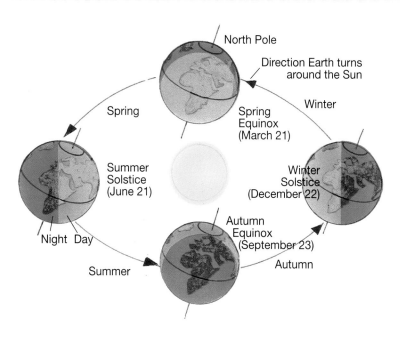

THE SEASONS
The earth turns around the Sun on a tilted axis. It gets more or less heat during the four different seasons of the year. In winter the Northern Hemisphere is tilted away from the Sun and its rays give less heat and it is cold. In summer it is tilted towards the Sun and gets more heat and it is hot.

THE MEDITERRANEAN CLIMATE
On the edges of the Mediterranean Sea the climate is made milder by the sea. Summers are hot and dry; winter is slightly rainy. Autumn and spring weather is changeable and more or less cool and humid.

THE TROPICAL CLIMATE
India is in a tropical zone. There are lots of heavy rain storms called monsoons in summertime. The air picks up moisture over the ocean and is pulled inland. The clouds cause torrential rain storms. Wind blows the other way in winter, towards the ocean. Winter is a dry season with occasional sudden heavy storms.

THE EQUATORIAL CLIMATE
Near the equator the seasons are very much the same. It is hot and damp all year long. Heavy rain falls every day during the summer on this village in the equatorial forest. Lots of clouds gather in the sky and can even cause tropical cyclones.

THE SUBTROPICAL CLIMATE IN AUSTRALIA
The climate is dry and sunny in Sydney on the southeast coast of Australia in the Southern Hemisphere.
The seasons are the opposite of ours. July is the coldest month in the middle of winter; it is usually about 55°F. It is summertime in December and the hottest month of the year is January (about 75°F).

THE WATER CYCLE

Water flows down mountains and goes to the sea in rivers. There the Sun's heat evaporates sea water which goes up and forms clouds in the sky. The water falls back to the earth as rain which fills the rivers and returns to the sea. This is the water cycle that causes climates to be more or less damp. In tropical climates more water evaporates and the cycle is the most active and creates monsoons.

Labels in the water cycle diagram: Precipitation (rain and snow), Mountains, Running Water, Ground Waters, Streams, Water Resurfaces, Rivers, Lake, River, Transpiration, Forest, Fields, City, The Sun's Rays, Evaporation, Sea

OCEANIC CLIMATE AT THE SOUTH POLE

It is winter at the South Pole in July. The polar night lasts 6 months from March to September. It gets colder as you move away from the coasts and can reach –95°F. A very strong wind blows in gusts of up to 180 miles per hour. It is warmest (14°F to –31°F) in December and January.

CONTINENTAL CLIMATE AT THE NORTH POLE

The climate is milder than at the South Pole. At the North Pole summer falls in the middle of a 6-month-long day because the Sun doesn't set. At midnight it brushes the horizon. This is called the midnight sun. Summer is short and cool (no more than 50°F) and lasts only three months. When the polar night (from September to March) begins, day starts at the South Pole.

ISBN 2-215-06162-6
© Éditions FLEURUS, Paris, 1998.
Printed in Italy.